MW00809511

Learn to Pray

In true prayer you experience God
True prayer makes you happy

Gabriele

The Word
The Universal Spirit

Gabriele Publishing House
P.O. Box 2221, Deering, NH 03244
(844) 576-0937
WhatsApp/Messenger: +49 151 1883 8742
www.Gabriele-Publishing-House.com

First Edition 2013
Published by:
© Universal Life
The Inner Religion
P.O. Box 3549
Woodbridge, CT 06525, U S A

Licensed edition
translated from the original German title:
"Lerne beten. Im wahren Gebet erlebst du Gott.
Wahres Beten macht glücklich"

From the Universal Life Series
with the consent of
© Gabriele-Verlag Das Wort GmbH
Max-Braun-Str. 2, 97828 Marktheidenfeld
Germany

Order No. S 174en
The German edition is the work of reference for all
questions regarding the meaning of the content.

Picture credits: front cover: © victoria p.-fotolia.
Back cover: © Martin-fotolia.

ISBN 978-1-890841-74-4

Preface

In a series of seminars, Gabriele, the prophetess and emissary of God in our time, taught from the divine Wisdom giving many specific and practical tips and exercises that can be applied in daily life, and in which lie the chance for a continuous spiritual growth.

Gabriele's explanations, which the seminar was based on entitled, "Learn to Pray. In True Prayer You Experience God. True Prayer Makes You Happy," are passed on in this book.

eople pray.

People request.

People hope.

People ask about God. Where is God? Does God hear me? Does God understand me? Does He love me? Well, is there a God at all? If God exists, why doesn't He speak up? Why doesn't He answer me?

Question after question!

Let us realize that the Christ of God and thus, the Spirit of our eternal Father, too, is nearer to us than our arms and legs.

If He is truly so near – why don't we hear Him?
Anyone who asks this question should ask himself: Is he oriented toward God, or has he turned away from God through his personal, egotistical aspects?

7

Why do many complain that they do indeed pray to God, but hardly get an answer from God – and if so, they don't know if it was the answer from the great Spirit of life.

We mostly direct the question in the word "why" to our fellowman or a theologian. Can our fellowman or the theologians give us answers, if they are not capable of hearing God in their innermost being themselves?

The "why," directed to people, leads to ever more riddles, because many a one whom we ask shrugs his shoulders and says: "I don't know why we don't hear God."

And the theologian will give us an answer something like the following: "We shouldn't be arrogant. The question of why we don't hear God belongs to the field of theology. These are, after all, the mysteries of God."

Why, why, why! The answer to our "why" is very simple. Instead of going toward God, we run away from Him.

Jesus taught us: "Ask, and it will be given to you; seek, and you will find; knock, and it will be opened to you."

Where should we turn to with our asking?

Where should we seek, and where knock?

Never with people nor with a theologian, because he, too, is merely a human being. Only when the individual realizes that he is the temple of God, himself, and that God dwells in him, will he know where he can turn to.

We have to learn to turn to within, to find God in us.

In prayer, spoken in our own inner being, we experience God.

But true prayer needs to be learned, because the right prayer, to pray in ourselves, is a dialogue with God.

Many people rattle off their prayers, but their thoughts are totally somewhere else, so, they're not with their prayers. These are prayers that are turned without.

Jesus said: "Ask, and it will be given to you ..." However, many people plead to God for this or that, and mostly it is personal things. God should fulfill our human desires, which are often an obstacle to the salvation of our soul.

*O*nly when a person finds his way to the right prayer of the deed, will this determine his life on Earth. Prayers of the deed are prayers strong in belief, which make us happy.

How do we find our way to prayers of the deed?

We will find our way to a true prayer of the deed only when we question our prayers of requests or thanks, when we check ourselves to see whether we are like what we are praying for.

Only when our prayer is a deep prayer, when we have learned to pray in the center of the power of the Christ of God and we feel along with our prayers, will we feel that we are suddenly carried by a power that is always present.

If we then fulfill our prayers in daily life, by filling our life with them and thus, doing the will of God, then we draw closer to the center of love, which is in us. We go toward God.

The step-by-step journey to within, to the eternal Spirit of love soon lets us sense that God, our Father in Christ, our Redeemer, comes several steps toward us.

Prayers of the deed, which we fulfill in our daily life, gradually become prayers of experience.

We learn, sense and experience how we become more aware of God's nearness, step by step.

In our daily life, we experience that God's love supports and helps us; we experience His presence in our feelings.

We become more peaceable.

We attain security and trust in God.

We approach our work more and more with God, we work with His power more and more, and experience Him in our daily life.

Suddenly, we understand our colleagues at work, for instance, and can help them, without showing off. In many situations, we notice and realize that God exists.

In many ways, which at first are still unknown to us, God answers us.

And so, let us first learn to become free from ourselves, from our thought patterns, which twine themselves around passion, hatred, envy, desires, cravings and much more.

All this embellishment permeates our feelings and our thoughts.

Our words are then also shaped by what we think, feel and want. This results in the unrest of our nervous system, which transmits itself to the whole person, who then revolves again and again around what's going on in his head. This is, as mentioned at the beginning, the turning away from God.

From this "state of being," we then ask the many questions: "Where is God?" "Why doesn't He hear me?" "Or does He understand me, after all?" "Does He perhaps not love me?" "Or does He love me, after all?"

Anyone who gets caught in his own embellishment is heading toward his self-made misfortune.

A saying goes:
"Everyone is the architect of his own fate!"
If we expand this statement, then it could be:
Everyone is the architect of his own misfortune, and ultimately, the perpetrator of all that hits him.
Most people, who mention again and again that they pray so much, are preoccupied with themselves, that is, they are spinning around

their personal affairs, thus hardly noticing how their neighbor is getting along.

Let us begin with ourselves, by asking the question: Can I relate to what I'm praying for in me, in my innermost being?
And, am I the person who does what he prays for in his daily life?

*L*et us realize:
Without empathy, without feeling into what we pray for, we will not reach God.

To draw closer to God in prayer, we must gradually become still.
We will become still only when we conquer ourselves with the power of the Christ of God, by clearing out what stands between God and us.

If we are willing to work on our all-too-human aspects with the Spirit of Christ, we will become calmer.

Our prayer will then first become a prayer of contemplation, which means that we contemplate all our prayer concerns with the question:
Do I act according to my prayers in daily life?

*F*or example, when we pray for people, animals, yes, for Mother Earth, we ask ourselves:
How do we act toward our fellowman? How do we feel with our animal brothers and sisters? And how do we sense the Mother Earth in us?

We have to learn to feel into our prayers, to gain empathy, so as to sense how things are, for instance, for the person for whom we are praying, for how our animal brothers and sisters feel, or even the Mother Earth.

We should first let all our concerns that we place before God reverberate in our inner being, feeling into the situations, in the awareness:

What I do not want someone to do to me should not be done to anyone else either, neither by me nor by my fellowman.

And so, I feel into the situations and tell myself: "I do not want to experience it this way." Based on this, we can pray for our neighbor with a certain amount of empathy.

In this way, we will very gradually find our way to true prayer.

In true prayer, in this deep empathy, which comes alive in us, we very soon notice that we are uplifted by a power that we did not know until now. We feel:

That is an answer from God.

It is the Spirit that touches us.

Our prayers of request and thanks are then prayers of experience. Nor do we struggle for words anymore. We sense how very gradually the prayers come from within; it is our soul, which is helping; it is beginning to pray with us.

*I*f we allow it to pray from within, then our prayers will become more genuine, more and more selfless prayers of request or deep concerns for our neighbor, for the Mother Earth.

Prayers that merely revolve around our personal, human concerns, around the benefits, the advantages for us, show a lack of trust in God, who knows about all things.

Prayers from the heart, prayers of experience or learning, prayers of empathy are not within the range of the confinement of human and all-too-human concerns. They are usually oriented to the great whole.
They are prayers for people, for souls in the spheres of purification, for people who die, for people who are born, for nature – many concerns for the great totality, in the awareness that the all-encompassing, universal power of God, His mighty radiation, always brings about what is good.

*L*et us realize that every prayer as a means to an end comes from the base nature of the all-too-human and is not heard by God.

The many questions about God, spoken by people who pray and receive no answer, indicate that their prayers are "distant prayers" because for these people God is far away. Such prayers find no resonance in the heart, because they are spoken to without, whereby the thoughts are in a totally different world, in the person's ego-world.

If we learn to value ourselves as a cosmic being, higher than our base ego, then we will gain distance from ourselves, from our egoistic behavior. Then our prayers will become deeper and more fervent.

The all-too-human separates us from God. Only when we have learned to refrain from complaints and self-accusations, will we feel that God is closer to us.

If we ask Him from our heart to help us over-come our all-too-humanness, then the help is also present.

The power of the Spirit helps us to conquer our-selves. We become calmer and turn to within more and more deeply, until we linger in the center of the Christ of God, which shines near our physical heart. Then our prayers are carried by the Spirit of love and we notice more and more: Our soul prays, the inner being, which we are in God.

Many people accuse themselves before God; it is the self-accusation that comes from the dissatisfaction with ourselves. Self-accusa-tion is always a lack of trust in God, the result of which is that God's consolation is slow in coming.

$\mathcal{M}$any people pray for God to support and help our fellowmen in their suffering, in their misfortune. Rarely do those praying ask themselves how great their empathy is for those for whom they are praying.

Only when a person has learned to feel into the suffering of his neighbor, when he has learned to sense this in the center of the Christ of God in himself, is he praying.

To the extent that we feel how it fares with our fellowman, for who we are praying, for what he has to bear, that is, when the woe and pain of the other resounds in us, can we say: We are praying.

A prayer without inner participation is not a prayer, but merely a stammering of prayer words.

And so, to pray for others means to feel into their suffering, their hardship, into their illness.

It has to pain us in our heart that the others are going through this. Only then are we able to send impulses of strength.

These genuine, deep impulses of strength, which flow from our prayer, positive, selfless thought energies, may help our neighbor to understand his suffering or even to bear it, or they help him to find his way in prayer to Christ, who is the helper, advisor and healer.

Whoever learns to entrust himself and his neighbor to God, that is, to pray from the heart with feeling and empathy, also feels in his own heart that his own evil or the evil of his neighbor is addressed by the power of the Christ of God, by the Inner Physician and Healer.

The consolation in our own heart and in that of our neighbor makes us happy. These are true, deep prayers of experience.

As soon as we feel embedded in God's love and wisdom, we will not ask for anything more for ourselves, for the prayer of the soul is a worship of God; from this flow impulses of strength for our fellowman.

The love for God and neighbor is the highest prayer. "Love your neighbor" means to understand him, to feel into him, and to sense how he is faring.
From this selfless prayer develops a dialogue with God.

*T*rue prayer also leads to spiritual maturity. Only when we experience the stillness of the inner being and the sublime happiness from our soul, do we know: That is God's answer.

Until we have attained this selfless prayer, we have to learn over and over again.

In prayer, we also need to sense the great unity, which, in turn, grows from the love for God.

Let us go into nature, and open our eyes wide and let nature move into our inner being!

Let us feel that every blade of grass, every bush, every mighty tree, every little animal and every mineral lives.
The sensing of life is, in turn, God's answer.

When we learn to live in this great unity, we feel that we are linked with all creatures, detached, that is, independent of time and space, eternal Being, which blossoms more and more under the sun of love.
That is life in the present. That makes us happy and free. That is true prayer.

And so, when we learn to pray, then we learn to live and thus, stand as a part of the great whole. Through this, we experience God's presence and His answer in manifold ways and means.

As long as we are stormy in our hearts, as long as our prayers are merely a prattling, we pray to without and ultimately feel the hollowness of our existence, which surrounds us, because God does not address us. He cannot touch us because, in reality, we have not turned to Him, we have not taken up, created, the connection to Him.

God comes closer to us only in our inner being, in our true, deep prayer.

And so, let us realize: Every external search for God is futile. A lip prayer also does not find assurance in the heart, either.

Only when we meet God in us while praying, do we feel the great, cosmic, state of Oneness, and we will experience God everywhere – however, not externally, but in everything that we encounter.

People are often afraid of all that could hit them. This makes them restless and draws them to without. Let us realize that nothing can hit us that we have not sent out, ourselves, that is, with which we have previously hit others. We prepare heaven and hell ourselves. Both are inner states of becoming aware, which we should be aware of in good time, in order to abstain from "hell." What we make of our life depends on us.

Our daily motto could be:
Be calm. Fight your turmoil with the power of the Christ of God, by clearing up whatever is moving you; for every state of turmoil in our thoughts and feelings makes us anxious, unfree, and doesn't allow us to become still and pray, aware of our feelings.

Our soul can rest in God only when we do not stir it up through our all-too-humanness.
When the Spirit of God can nurture our soul because we have become still, then we feel the "sustenance" of the inner being; it is the tran-

quility in the person, the stillness, the oneness with infinity. That is our true being. We will achieve this only when daily, we learn, learn, learn – when we learn to pray.

*M*any church Christians have forgotten how to pray.
Is this also true for us? When we look into our world, we have to admit to ourselves that people in the western world may call themselves Christian, but are very far from truly being Christian. The so-called Christians have mostly become parroters. They parrot the prayers, for instance, that were led by church officials. They have forgotten to live their prayers.

In the present time, we experience the excesses of a sham-Christianity, the so-called hatred of foreigners, instead of brotherly love. Sham-Christianity demands a religious creed instead of recognition, in order to walk in the footsteps of Jesus, the Christ.

*I*n the prayer of experience, of feeling into and empathizing, we become more sensitive. When it is wanted, we will then offer a helping hand to people, to help and serve them from our own spiritual experience.

If this is not yet possible for us, because we may be against our neighbor, then we should not give him or other fellowmen any good advice.

Anyone who is not able to give inner comfort from his own inner, spiritual, life substance, cannot instruct any person, either, so that he may find the way to inner stillness, where the inner guide, advisor, helper and healer waits for him.

Let us think about what this means:
Prayer and living should form a unity.

$\mathcal{M}$any people rely on people and are disappointed over and over again.

A person who does not depend on people, but on the other hand, asks the Eternal for help, advice and support, cannot be forsaken by any person either, because he does not rely on people, but on Christ, the eternal Spirit, who is present in all things.

Particularly during the present time, we should realize that God is in all things, that God's heart beats in everything and that we should take root and live in the very basis of the Eternal.

When we strive for this in prayer, then we will become happy from within and feel united with the great Spirit.

Whoever turns within in prayer and senses in his heart his neighbor, yes, all of infinity, has the power to open the inner gate to the kingdom of the Spirit of God.

When we have found God in our hearts through true prayer, which we should practice and cultivate, then we feel Him everywhere as the omnipresent, good, friendly, loving One, the Spirit of love.

Then we experience that God looks at us from every person, every flower, bush and tree, from every mineral.
From every sound of an animal, from the wind, the rays of the sun, from every drop of water and from each grain of sand, we then experience the almighty radiation, the Almighty, and we are not alone; we are united with Him and surrounded by the might of love.

Let us learn to pray in our inner being, in the true prayer of experience, by feeling into and empathizing, in concern for all that surrounds us, what we see and don't see, and for all people, beings and life forms. Then we will walk the path to life, for God is the All-life.
Our days are then light-filled, permeated by the inner sun. We experience God when we awaken – He is with us.

At each moment we experience that God is with us. In the evening, when we retire, we feel: The great stillness is with us, GOD.
Let us learn to live as immortal beings, only then will we live.

$\mathcal{M}$any a one asks himself:
Do I pray in the right way?
Do I pray in such a way that Christ hears me, that He understands me?

We could do an exercise, to learn to find ourselves.

First, what would we do, for instance, when the picture on our television is distorted? The first question is surely: Has the antenna been moved? Is the satellite dish no longer properly oriented? We will very quickly call an expert and have him adjust the antenna or satellite dish, so that a good, clear picture can be seen on the screen again.

Each one of us is also sender and receiver. And in each one of us come the corresponding pictures, according to our inner orientation, our attitude toward life.

Thus, we human beings are like an antenna that needs to be oriented. Externally, we could accept a help for this: It is an upright meditative posture.

When we let ourselves slump comfortably into a chair or an armchair, for instance, then the antenna is not oriented to God. To turn within, we have to assume an attitude toward the inner life; then we will feel that several things fall into place in us.

In general, we should adopt this Christian posture in our daily life, but very consciously in prayer.
We should make our body as light as possible, to be able to receive the impulses of inner life. That's why this exercise.

We are accustomed to leaning on the chair; actually that's why the backrest is there. But what if we only lean on it with our tailbone, that is, if we sit up straight?

And so, try to support only the tailbone with the backrest. Both feet are next to each other on the floor.
Our spinal column supports our head, upright and straight.
And now we feel into ourselves.
We notice that something changes.

Now we direct our attention to our right hand.
We place the palm of our left hand on the back of our right hand, palms up.
Many of us know where the center of Order pulsates. It pulsates near the tailbone, the coccyx.
We turn both hands, placed in one another, the left palm lying on the right hand, toward the center of Order, that is, toward the body.
In this posture, we pray for ourselves personally. We take up contact with the great Spirit in us.

We can close our eyes, so that we feel our body better.

We feel that our outer, and thus, our inner, posture is different than usual. We feel that we are prepared to pray.

Now we turn to within.
We turn to the Christ of God in us, the Christ-light near our physical heart.

We draw our senses to within, in order to sense how our thoughts withdraw from us.
We also feel that our breathing is deeper.

We feel that we become calmer.
We sense that head and heart become a unit, for it becomes calm in us.

We do not accept any thoughts.
Our breathing is now calm and deep.

Now we pray for our concerns.

We do not seek for words of prayer.
We let the prayer thoughts come and take them into the Christ-light that shines near our physical heart.

Prayer thoughts develop.
Now, in the light of Christ, in the Christ center, we try to pray.

We take our time. We are learning to pray.

We feel that our body is now a lot lighter, on the one hand, through the meditative sitting posture, the prayer posture, on the other hand, by praying in the Christ-light in us.

I may now bring you back from this exercise, for the next exercise.

We remain in this prayer posture.

In our thoughts, we now want to pray for our fellow people, for the animals, for nature.

Let us again realize that we are senders and receivers.
We have just received for ourselves – now we pray for our fellow people, for nature and animals, for what is near and dear to us.

For this, we open ourselves.
We place the backs of both hands on our thighs and draw them somewhat close to our body.

Let us again feel the lightness of our body. It now begins to vibrate very softly in the palms of our hands. This is saying that the soul wants to give. The light in us and in our soul wants to carry the prayer out to our fellow brothers and sisters, to all life forms.

We turn within again.

We draw our senses within and imagine the Christ-light near our heart. It pulsates and shines harmoniously.

Now, we bring to the Christ of God our prayer concerns for our neighbor, for nature, for animals, for Mother Earth.

We ask Christ, for people, for the various life forms.

We place these prayers of petition in the pulsating Christ-power and remain praying in this inner power.

It prays, for prayer thoughts come. We do not search for prayer words, we let them come.

The prayers of petition flow through our body. They flow to without. Via the palms of our hands, via our fingertips, they go to the people for whom we pray, to the life form that we remembered in prayer.

By way of the Christ of God center in us, the power flows through us to our neighbor.
Wherever we direct our prayers to – if they are a genuine concern, our fellowmen or the life forms, for who we have prayed, will receive.

I may now bring us back again from this prayer practice.

We close the prayer circle again, by again placing our left palm facing up, under the back of the right hand.
We again direct both hands, which we have placed in each other, toward the center of Order.

A circulation of energy begins to flow in us.
This circulation of spiritual power becomes tangible: We breathe more calmly. We are more concentrated. We feel lighter and fresher. We sense the nearness of the Christ of God.

I may bring you back from the exercise.

*I*n many a one of us thoughts came, from which he could not free himself, which beset him during prayer. If possible, we should analyze these thoughts before praying, that is, question them, to then clear them up. Through this, we become calmer and then find our way increasingly into deep prayer, into the prayer of experience, that is, of recognition.

When we pray in a calm and reflective prayer, we sense an inner depth. We do not struggle for prayer words; from our soul flow fine prayer feelings that flow by way of our brain and trigger certain prayer requests or prayer thoughts for our neighbor. On the other hand, if something is bothering us, if we feel the unrest even in prayer, then we realize that our subconscious is active, that thoughts want to come, which we perhaps push away. The unrest that makes itself noticeable when we sit down to pray, that is, when we want to pray, always shows that something is waiting – perhaps already for a long time – to be cleared up.

Basically, it is desirable that such thoughts bother us when we want to pray; they indicate that something should have been cleared up long since.

During our work or our activity, thoughts run automatically, often without our being aware of them. But when we withdraw to pray, they literally assault us. This indicates that our soul wants to be freed from this evil.

But it is also possible that precisely when we want to pray, the subconscious speaks up and interferes with all our good intentions. Then we should not say: "I'll push these thoughts aside, because now I want to pray!" Instead, we say: "Oops! What's waiting to be dealt with? I will immediately analyze and clear it up!"

It would not be advisable to simply write down our pressing and obsessive thoughts, as it were, and then put the note aside, in order to align ourselves anew and decide: "But now I go into prayer impersonally!"

Rather, we should first become aware of the content of these thoughts, striving to rectify with Christ what we have recognized in and on ourselves.

We assume our upright prayer posture, but this time with the intention to now pray for ourselves. In prayer, we then ask Christ to support and help us to clear up these thoughts, which we have questioned, and in which we recognize our ego components – if we want this.

That is important! We have to want to do this, and we have to feel bad about it. There has to be a certain amount of pain there, that we are still the way the content of our thoughts shows us. If this is so, then, however, we also sense the help.

It can take place as follows: We want to pray. A still diffuse unrest doesn't really let us become still. We consciously allow the negative aspect that moves us to form into thoughts, which we can grasp. If our disturbing thoughts and feelings are not serious, not obsessive, we note them down. They will then keep their distance when we turn to Christ with our request. We then become calmer and can, as foreseen, pray deeply.

Afterward, after our prayer, we should clear up what was in our thoughts, in the pressing thoughts, for example, against our fellowman. If we have sinned against an aspect of nature, then we clear this up with the great Spirit, the Creator-Spirit of nature. Then we firmly resolve to no longer nurture such thoughts or to no longer do what our thoughts have urged us to again and again.

*I*mportant is the prayer, again and again, the request for help to Christ, who dwells in us. He supports and helps us, providing that we want to become free of these wrong attitudes. That is decisive.

To truly learn to pray, honesty toward ourselves is necessary. Each day is not like the others. Let us critically observe ourselves:

At the moment we search for prayer thoughts, we are searching in our head, in our subconscious. We should then recognize that we are repressing thoughts and becoming tense.

So if problematic thoughts assail you while praying, do not repress them! Look at them, for they show themselves in pictures. Write them down, and then – when you have become calmer – go into prayer.

Ask Christ for support and help to recognize and clear up these all-too-human aspects, we would also say, the sins or the wrong attitudes.

We strive to become calmer. We want to find our way into the inner stillness, to be able to pray from the heart, for true prayer is a dialogue with God. It makes us happy; it makes us strong in faith; it makes us more secure in everyday life. Why? Because we sense His presence.

Why do many, many thoughts break in over us, often, exactly when we want to pray?

Let us bring to mind that much lies in our sub-conscious that we have repressed in the way of desires, claims and ambitions – also guilt and other things that burden us, because we did not want to admit to it in our conscious mind.

These negative energies are stored in our sub-conscious and from there encroach upon our feelings, sensations, thoughts and actions. We should figure out these inputs, so that we are able to deal with them, to clear them up and become free of them.

If we now resolve to pray, that is, if we strive to become calmer, then our subconscious reacts immediately.

It uses the chance to assail us – with whatever it wants, because, by all means, our subcon-scious wants to put through what we bear, un-acknowledged, in ourselves, as all-too-human desires.

And so, if thoughts assail us, we write them down.

We ask the Spirit for help and support, so that we can clear them up.

I repeat: If we want this – and fulfill what we have recognized. Should these thoughts appear again, we do not allow it.

Once more, we ask for help: "Lord, I have asked You to transform these aspects. Now I place these thoughts at Your feet and ask You to help me to no longer harbor these thoughts!"

Let us go within again and again, let us go into meditative prayer, and we will experience that Christ supports us. We sense the Spirit in us. This feeling and sensing makes us happy and glad from within. We can approach our fellow-man in a much calmer and balanced way and also achieve more in daily life. A person who is ready and willing to rectify the all-too-human aspects with His help feels better from day to day.

First is the prayer of recognition and then the prayer of the deed.

The prayer of the deed means that we feel in our heart: It is a genuine concern that all goes well for people, nature and animals. We will judge less and less often, that is, disparage others or be envious. These ambitions of the all-too-humanness recede more and more, because we are working with the power of the Christ of God. Our soul becomes more light-filled, our person freer. This means that given time, the soul will pray.

The prayer from the depths of our soul is a profound prayer of thanks, a selfless prayer, which makes us glad and happy, from our soul. It is an inner joy, because as a person we also sense that we have drawn closer to God.

But it requires practice; it is a constant learning. Please do not give up! Practice over and over again; pray again and again, until it becomes a very deep desire to act in daily life as our prayers are. Through this, we become creative; we draw from the power of life, which is in us.

*S*omeone who is truly vivified by the desire to find himself and to draw closer to Christ is also willing to learn.

The one who wants to, gathers experiences on how the various sitting positions have an effect on him and in him.

For instance, slouching in a chair – which thoughts come? And what is it like when you consciously hold yourself upright, resting on your tailbone? Watch yourself, and remember this often.

The prayer posture, which we have already addressed – sitting upright with both feet on the floor – it, too, wants to be learned. I can say from my own experience: When you also assume this posture during conversations, it is much easier for you to listen to your neighbor and give him the right answer. You then find the lawful solution much more quickly and surely, also in your work area.

Leaning against the wall, for example, or against doorjambs also shows us that we are not concentrated. We cannot fully focus on our neighbor or a situation, because leaning against the doorjamb or wall is already based on thoughts that have brought us into this position.

We have gotten to know a prayer posture that is useful and beneficial for the collection of our powers of consciousness.

Many a one has noticed that we fall back again all-too-easily, even though we've resolved to do it differently.

But we should also experience what it is like when we slouch in a chair, what thoughts develop. Are these the deep prayer thoughts linked with God? We learn that we can never pray intensely this way.
We do have prayer thoughts, but as we ourselves sense, they come from without. These are, then, externalized prayers – prattling prayers. Between these prayer tracts lie our desires, thoughts that entirely possess us. Let us try it;

let us make our own experiences; then we will learn.

It was not without reason that Christ said to us in many revelations, in which the goal was to receive His radiation: "Assume an inner and outer posture."

On the Inner Path, the path to the inner life, the conscious, aligned, ultimately, disciplined posture is a very, very great help. For one thing, to find oneself, for another, to recognize more clearly and quickly which thoughts go out from us during the course of our day. With the power of our Redeemer, we can also overcome what we clearly recognize in and on ourselves as negative aspects.

The spiritually conscious, upright posture bears witness to respect, straightforwardness and a certain inner strength. This posture is an inner humility before the great Spirit, a thankfulness toward Him.

Let us always remember the antenna. The human being is also sender and receiver.

It would be a gain for us if we discipline our-selves and apply this upright spiritual posture toward ourselves, by making ourselves aware again and again of whom we actually are. For example: Am I merely a listless human being? Or is there in me a power before which I should assume a correct posture? If we are aware of this, then we will also do it.

*L*et us make the experience, ourselves! In daily life, for instance, during a conversation or on the telephone, we can clearly notice this: If we orient our antenna, then we sense how we receive help from within. If we were tired, for example, suddenly more strength flows to us. This takes place due to the orientation, which we gradually adhere to, totally as a matter of course – if we have learned it. We become en-tirely different people. We learn to truly pray. We learn to deal with our neighbor in a good way. We are happier. We grow closer to our neighbor from within – and much more.

The upright posture helps. Through a conscious alignment with Christ, we truly take a great step forward.

We sense what it means: "The Kingdom of God is in us" or "I am the temple of God."
From this grows the desire to cleanse our temple, in order to become free, in order to attain the inner feeling "God is present."

Over and over again, let us make ourselves aware:
The human being is merely the shell of the great, light-filled being. The light-filled being in us should radiate throughout the shell.

Recommended Reading

Inner Prayer

Heart Prayer
Soul Prayer
Ether Prayer
Healing Prayer

Many people think that the material world and the spiritual world are far apart from each other. In reality, the coarse, material spheres of existence on Earth are closely connected with the ethereal spheres. They are levels of vibration that exist next to each other and at the same time. For this reason, we can very well live in this world without being with this world. We have only to decide to give preference to the inner reality of all being, to the divine...

"The one who daily prays in the right way, from the heart, will also keep the inner peace in the greatest uproar..."

96 pgs., Order No.S 307en, $ 5.00

To order a free catalog or book:
Universal Life, The Inner Religion
P.O. Box 3549, Woodbridge, CT 06525, U S A
www.universal-spirit.org
Tel. 1-800-846-2691

The
Ten Commandments
of God
Through Moses
Interpreted with
present-day words

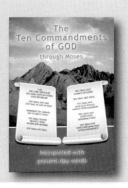

The Ten Commandments of God through Moses are a gift of love from the Eternal to His human children, a help for their life. They are excerpts from the all-encompassing eternal law of infinity. The life is God, the free Spirit, which is one and the same in all cultures worldwide. The free Spirit in all cultures worldwide is the unending diversity and fullness of the Being. Each Commandment of God is a gateway to the fullness of life because God, the free Spirit, is the life.

44 pgs., Order No. S338en, $ 3.00

Free Booklets

Don't Let Go!
A Small Gift For You

"Don't Let Go!" – These are three words spoken into our heart. They have a very deep meaning for those people who believe in a higher power that dwells in us, that is able to give strength, help and support in abundance. It means to hold on tight to the One who dwells in you, in all of us: the free Spirit of love.
"Don't Let Go" helps to find an inner balance, to attain calm and harmony, through which we may experience that God is present.

28 pgs., Order No. G328en

To order a free catalog or book:
Universal Life, The Inner Religion
P.O. Box 3549, Woodbridge, CT 06525, U S A
www.universal-spirit.org
Tel. 1-800-846-2691

God In Us!

God in us, God in you, God in me – each one of us is the temple of God and God dwells in us. And so, the immortal life, the breath of God, is in the very basis of our soul. Life streams through our soul. It streams into our cell body and we breathe the life. Our heart beats because it receives the life from the all-encompassing life, God.

God is always present. He is in nature. He is the life; He is the light in every animal, in every stone, in every mighty tree. God is in the very basis of your soul. God is with you and by you.

20 pgs., Order No. G318en

Free Booklets -
"The Message of Truth"

Small reading gems, excerpts from the divine Wisdom that give you something to think about:

Help for the Sick and Suffering – *G307en*

You Are Not Alone – *G303en*

A Fulfilled Life into Old Age – *G306en*

The Sermon on the Mount – The Path to a Fulfilled Life – *G304en*

You Live Eternally – There Is No Death – *G309en*

Pearls of Life for You – *G302en*

Comfort in Need and Suffering – *G308en*

Reincarnation – Life's Gift of Grace – *G310en*

Gabriele Publishing House
P.O. Box 2221, Deering, NH 03244
(844) 576-0937
WhatsApp/Messenger: +49 151 1883 8742
www.Gabriele-Publishing-House.com